Book title: "The frogs and the dog

Written by: Abiygayil C. Yisrael

The frogs and the dog copyright 2018, by (Pearl) Abiygayil C. Yisrael

If any questions or feedbacks, please contact me at; or yisrael.pearl@gmail.com or circle-of-love@hotmail.com either it doesn't matter.

<u>Acknowledgement</u>:

I would like to praise my heavenly Father Yahwa for given me such great talent; for that, I am able to produce the seed that can feed the needs of the minds with laughter, joy and love; so, thank you Yahwa, God Almighty, for being such blessing to me; plus, to the world.

<u>Dedication</u>:

I dedicate this book here to my heavenly Father Yahwa, Love himself, first; then to the world.

Introduction:

Shalom, hi and aloha, my name is Abiygayil Chephtsiybah Yisrael, and you guys can call me Pearl, now the thing is this, I am writing this piece here, because I want the little ones to have something to enjoy; to feel that they have something valuable to look for. this is the reason, I am producing this seed of laughter; joy for all boys and girls. And so, I am coming to a close here, I just hope you all find it to be fun and also loving. And so, without a moment to waste or to lose here is my story lines coming at you all...and so, here it goes, I will start by saying this, once upon a time there was a little boy name James, who loves to go outdoors, to collect frogs, whether they were under the log; or on the log James would go and catch them one way; or another, no matter the weather he got to be out there; he has no <u>fear</u>, I <u>swear</u> when it comes to the doing what he loves to do. And so, when little James goes out to enjoy nature itself, it's like he is on another planet; or world, therefore, he doesn't want to be bothered at all. Whether, he <u>falls</u>, <u>crawls</u>; also <u>run</u>. But he got to have his <u>fun</u> especially when the <u>sun</u> is <u>out</u> and <u>about</u> that is like a gold mine to him. But anyway, as I continue telling the <u>story</u>, I hope at the end I gets the <u>glory</u>, for telling a good <u>story</u>. Ha! Ha!... I am enjoying this, and as I move <u>along</u> and not <u>prolong</u> too <u>long</u>, little James rush to his quest collecting his frogs from one side to another, getting himself in a <u>mess</u>, but trust me, he is not <u>stress</u>, not all. For he is having a ball as he rolls, <u>jump</u>, <u>stump</u> and <u>bump</u> into things; even over things.... he's doing his thing because this is what he loves to do, anything that's concerns <u>nature</u> and he is pretty <u>mature</u> about this, his mom; dad can't even stop him when it comes to his first love; and what is his first love? Nature, and then comes his food...but nothing else comes first. But just that. And so, along the way, when little James was on his way home, he thought he saw a big dog standing looking a far, to where he was standing <u>while</u> checking his jar of frogs; being captivated by these little rubbery cold blooded amphibians, and no! I did not say <u>crocodile</u>, but what I did say, is amphibian, and he is all <u>out</u>; <u>about</u> there in the wild, man...that little <u>child</u> is something else. But gnarly, it keeps him smiling and excited base on what he has accomplish every day. And so, as he stopped and looked at his little rubbery amphibian friends there, in the jar he saw the big dog keep staring at him; so, in his mind... he was frightening because the dog was too <u>big</u> and it reminds him of a <u>pig</u>. But anyway, far as James is concern the dog is like a monster to him; so, he started to run off, hurrying to get home, to get away from this beast, monster that scared him practically out of his <u>wits</u>, as he <u>splits</u> and didn't <u>quit</u> up until he got home, and there he was safe. So thank God for his speed, and now he doesn't have to <u>worry</u> and

or be <u>sorry</u> about not trying to get away from

this dog, that actually isn't harmful at all, he is

pretty friendly, but little James didn't take his

<u>time</u> to <u>find</u> that out, he just wanted out, be out

of <u>sight</u> and that was <u>quite</u> <u>alright</u> and with him;

that was the end of this confrontation...at least

for now. As well as now, as you guys follows me, it

is next day, and James is up again, ready for

another <u>adventure</u> to meet up with <u>nature</u> and the

little rubbery <u>creatures</u>, that is a <u>dear</u> to him,

for without them in his life to <u>share</u> his love with

them, he would be <u>down</u> and clearly with a <u>frown</u>,

but since that is not the case, he is happy as a

lurk. Going to spend the time; day with what he

loves best, and you all guys already know what he is about to do. And that is... to look and collect some more <u>frogs</u> to see if they are hiding under the <u>logs</u>; also on top of them. For the <u>frogs'</u> love jumping and <u>bouncing</u>, <u>unannounced</u> at times, whether on <u>log</u> or not, little James comes out to catch them as he fetches them in his <u>jar</u>, it's almost like the frogs are behind <u>bars</u>, but just in a glass jar bottle, in fact he has them in there, he doesn't want them to escape without him releasing them, so to play it safe, he rather contains them in the locked jar with little holes being poked on the top of the glass jar. And quite frankly, my dear, little ones.... James likes them in the clear jar so he can look at them, at every chance that he gets because he loves them, I guess in some cases, it brings some kind of pleasure to him. When they are around. And so, James did go <u>out</u> and <u>scout</u> and enjoyed his day in the sun by the lake with Tyler, Rick, Rex, Dixie, Daisy, Lisa, Brownie; also, Samuel that is the names of his little frogs and as the day ends, James headed home with no catch today, but either way, for now James was content with the ones he has at hand; so, little James was not vex to the point that he did get anything, for in his mind there is always <u>tomorrow</u>, as long he doesn't <u>sorrow</u>, it'll be alright. So as he got home, he called his mom to see where she was...there she was, waiting for him and as he approached his mom, he said hey mom, I didn't catch anything today, but it's okay, every day I go out there, doesn't mean I am going to be lucky; the mom hugs him, and told him that's the spirit, never give up, because there are days like that… you will face; so it is best to have a positive outlook on life; also on things. Then she grabs him, and told him to go in and take a shower, for few minutes; not an hour and James said okay mom, so what are we going to eat for dinner this evening? For you know…your food is always a winner, for I love the way you spice up the food and it certainly taste so good. (and the mother smiled at him and looked away, as James went on to take a shower.

Twenty-two minutes later. James was out of the

shower.... clean as a whistle and smelling all good and off he went to the kitchen to see if his mother Mary was in there, but Mary was in the living room watching television; little James came up and join her to keep her company and as quickly he sat down, quickly he fell asleep. Then Mary took her quilt and cover him, he looks so adorable; peaceful in that <u>state</u>, and the mother said what.... I <u>hate</u> to see him, awakes up too soon. I hope that is not the case....so she let him sleep right on the couch and turn off the television.

Two hours later, James was back up; sitting up with the look on his face, I wonder what is going on at the <u>spot</u> today, wanted to give it a <u>shot</u>, but Mary came in the living room and said, oh! You're up now….and what are you up to…little boy? OH nothing ma…just thinking of Dad; so when is he coming back from <u>Chicago?</u> Oh, can we <u>go,</u> there and see him? Mary replied, sure we can go there, if you like…and James said but when mother? And Mary replied how about next month on the 15th, me and you can arrange the trip and everything then we'll take it from there, and surprise daddy okay son? Then he replied okay ma, it's a good <u>ideal</u> for <u>real</u>. In addition, Mary said to James no outside for you today, maybe tomorrow, okay. Because you need to chill out a little bit, you squirt (Mary rubbed James head and turn on the television to cartoons, though James was a little disappointed but he understood after a while).

Next day, in the morning of course, the sun was up and shining so bright, with the birds chirping away, and while they was doing that, James slipped away, without even telling his mom that he left, just rushed by the lake, to his favorite spot, and as he was heading there, he happen to see the big dog again, just standing and staring at him, just as he was about to get real close to the lake, James got <u>scared</u>, and <u>stared</u> at the dog as well, wondering what to do next, should he run and scream or be quiet and step backwards real slowly so the dog wouldn't notice that he is trying to slip away quietly; while he was contemplating of what to do....the big dog looked like he wanted to come over towards him, but James dropped his jar and kindly run with his hands up in the air, screaming mommy, mommy, until he got back home, and run straight to his room. And there, his mother hurry up and rush to his aid, and asked him what happen, he was kind of out breath and unable to speak at that moment, he felt tormented by the dog, and Mary said calm down, what happen? He said I saw a big dog, it was a monster, and Mary had a strange look on her face, as if... wondering what is James talking about. But Mary continued to tell James to calm down, and he steady talking...it was a big dog mommy, I saw him and he was looking at me, I don't know what he was going to do to me. So I run...and run....and run until I got home and run in my <u>room</u>. So Mary, comfort little James and told him not to go back out there, until she is planning to go with him, James didn't look too <u>thrill</u> looked a little <u>ill</u> on the face, but worst case scenario... he had to <u>chill</u> because at this point momma was <u>right</u>; so, he couldn't <u>fight</u> her on that, so he just said okay; laid there on his bed. And said sorry to his mother, she hugged him; plus, kiss him on the forehead and asked him do he wants something to drink.... he said sure mom, I do. So, Mary brought him something nice and cool to <u>drink</u> while he lay there and <u>think.</u> And that made him to <u>think</u> about of what could have happen today, if he didn't <u>run</u>. Actually, James didn't find today to be so <u>fun</u> because of the big dog he had encountered on his path on his way to his favorite spot. Anyway, as the day rolls on; also by…. James was home playing with his toys, and while he was doing that, he taught that he heard a sound outside and he went off to check it out so going towards the kitchen's window he taught he saw the same big dog in his yard so he peeked in the window to make sure, and Walla! There he was just standing in the yard looking around, while sniffing too, so James yelled and called his mother…. besides Mary said what now! James, mom the big dog, the monster is in the yard and he's coming to get me, mommy……look, look he's here, in our yard. And Mary replied James get away from there, and let it alone, but…. but…but mom, he's getting closer to the kitchen's door; where are you James? I am still in the house, but in the kitchen, alright! Alright! I am coming right this minute, to put an end to this madness that has you all uptight, once and for all. Okay James where is he? (Mary looked out the window and saw him, and said wow! This is actually a big dog for real, I see why you are afraid of him, James, pass me the broom so I can chase him away out of our yard. And James says okay, mommy... I'll get the <u>broom</u> from my <u>room</u> fast. So Mary says hurry James, hurry! Before he leaves, then here comes James with the broom and gave it to his mom and Mary didn't hesitated and rush towards the dog with the broom, making noise and the big dog didn't budge, but just watch Mary coming his way; as she was coming his way, Mary happen to slip and fall on her face, worst case scenario the big dog came to Mary's rescue; when he got there, Mary was scared hoping that the big dog, don't bite her, but she comes to find out that he wasn't a harmful at all; so he started licking her face to remove the dirty on her skin, and when Mary saw that, she smiled and rub the big dog on his head, and say you are alright, but as for James, he was very afraid for his mom, hoping she doesn't get hurt by the monster he call him, but as he continue to look, he saw that the dog didn't mean any <u>harm</u>, for he was full of <u>charm</u>; was pretty <u>warm</u> towards his mom, and so he got <u>calm</u> and run outside as well, and as he was running towards his mom and the dog he happen to have pick up his jar of frogs he even <u>fell</u> as <u>well</u>, and the jar of frogs <u>popped</u> open and they all, the frogs of course <u>hopped</u> out, hopping their way to James mom as well, well...that is pretty <u>swell</u> for all of them heading towards Mary and the big dog's way and before you know it, the frogs <u>hopped</u> on the big dog's back all eight of them, and when James got to his mom he was smiling, too happy to see and know that his mom was okay; safe and that, the big dog that he call a monster was alright as well. As a result, Mary hugged the dog, the dog wiggled his tail, and Mary said to James.... hey he is alright James, looks like we got ourselves a dog now, besides the frogs and so, how do you like it now? And little James replied it is great ma, I am so loving it, it's like we are one big happy family and friends now. So Mary laugh and laugh and said oh, my god I really thought that dog was harmful, but I come to find out that he is a sweetheart, oh bless his heart, I am glad that we have met him and now you can stop running from him. So, what do you say about that? Find a name for our dog… okay, James say, how about Tyrell mom? Do you like it? And replied, sure, I couldn't think of a better name to call him. Good job James, my little man, and off they went inside the home, and brought Tyrell in as well, now Tyrell has a new home; also new friends and family too. And Mary said to James, now you don't need me, because you got Tyrell to go to your favorite spot now with you. He can protect you from <u>danger</u>; also <u>strangers</u> wouldn't you say, James? (James, jumped up and down and said yes of course ma, and you no longer have to worry about me anymore, now that I have Tyrell I could go enjoy myself, and also nature as well, now I feel well; and also pretty <u>swell</u>, and no more <u>hell</u>, because Tyrell is my friend now. And so, Mary said I thank God for sending Tyrell our way, for this a relief this day; so, go out and play James, for my worries are no more. So I praise God Love himself, Yahwa for being such a blessing, while he teaches us a lesson, for after all, this is where our blessings stem from, by learning of him; also lessons. And as I am coming to a close there, I would like to say, I hope all of you have enjoyed my story while God gets the glory, and this is the end of my story called the frogs and the dog. So, now that I have done that, I am pleased to let my heavenly Father, God Almighty Yahwa, Love himself to talk and to speak and make his comment on this book here; so, without a moment to lose, Father Yahwa please and come on in, say and share your piece concerning this work here; so forth. Okay, shalom, shalom, my little ones, and my lovely daughter (Pearl) Abiygayil Yisrael, I, Pops, God himself, Yahwa Love Myself is happy to say I am grateful; plus thankful for my daughter here, Abiygayil for allowing me to come on in; plus to join her on this project here; there, that she had in mind to present and plus to bring forth; about, that is; was very thoughtful of her to do so, and babe I am so very proud of you and your work there, I think it is awesome, and wonderful that the children of mines; also of all ages can enjoy and plus be able to relate too. However, it is pretty comical, excited, enjoyable; also well thought of and fix the kids, the little ones more so to enjoy with joy, I myself is really enjoying this piece of work here, that material is helpful; as well readable and also pretty incredible I can say, thanks babe, Pearl Abiygayil my one of my lovely angels of love with love to present such lovable and adorable books for kids that's the least I thought she wouldn't have done, but she surprised me, I, God Almighty Yahwa-YHWH, didn't think children's book would've been in her mind, but she went there and I am glad she did. And so, Pearl, they will enjoy your book there, because it is pretty interesting; and that...it was a cute title that you handpicked there; and also, came up with, and I didn't have nothing to do with it. But anyhow, babe Pearl Abiygayil with the twirl you have my blessings to go forth with that, the book of course. For you have made me so proud of how you went about and do it, the letters are cartoonish like... which is a good thing, and the size of it, is also great. What children wouldn't like this? And I'm God and the adult who enjoys this, and I am so loving it. good luck babe and be happy for your accomplishments, for I am happy for you too as well... I love you and thank you again for letting me, Pops, God Almighty, Yahwa the God of Heavens, to come on forth and say my piece concerning your work there. And this where I come to a halt, so though I come to a halt, you don't stop you keep going....and going, alright babe, I say shalom, Selah with love. Your God, Yahwa, the God; Father of heaven who art in heaven. (Pearl Abiygayil) okay, Pops God Almighty, I would also, like to say to you...thank you as well for giving me the opportunity to bring forth my skill to the forefront for all to witness; also to enjoy.

For if it wasn't for you God I wouldn't have been able to do this. But because of your divine mind, skills; as well, insights and wits, I was; and I am able to do so much and at the same time, I am able to shine so bright and show what is on my mind at the end of the evening. I am just so sorry to have waited the last minute to do this, when all along I had this skill in my hand. And so, Pops, God Almighty Yahwa- YHWH thank you for everything under the sun and also over the heavens, I love you and shalom.